Martin Luther King, Jr. Day

Rebecca Rissman

Heinemann Library
Chicago, Illinois

www.heinemannraintree.com
Visit our website to find out
more information about
Heinemann-Raintree books.

To order:

☎ Phone 888-454-2279

💻 Visit www.heinemannraintree.com
to browse our catalog and order online.

©2011 Heinemann Library
an imprint of Capstone Global Library, LLC
Chicago, Illinois

Edited by Adrian Vigliano and Rebecca Rissman
Designed by Ryan Frieson
Picture research by Tracy Cummins
Leveling by Nancy E. Harris
Originated by Capstone Global Library Ltd.
Printed in China by South China Printing Company Ltd.

15 14 13 12 11
10 9 8 7 6 5 4 3

Library of Congress Cataloging-in-Publication Data
Rissman, Rebecca.
  Martin Luther King, Jr. Day / Rebecca Rissman.
      p. cm.—(Holidays and festivals)
  Includes bibliographical references and index.
  ISBN 978-1-4329-4055-3 (hc) —ISBN 978-1-4329-4074-4 (pb) 1.
Martin Luther King, Jr., Day—Juvenile literature. 2. King, Martin Luther,
Jr., 1929-1968—Juvenile literature. I. Title.
  E185.97.K5R574 2011
  394.261—dc22   2009052855

Acknowledgments

The author and publishers are grateful to the following for permission to
reproduce copyright material: AP Photo/stf **p.8**; Corbis ©Louie Psihoyos/
Science Faction **p.6**; Corbis ©Bettmann **pp.7, 9, 15, 20, 23 top**;
Corbis ©Marvin Koner **p.10**; Corbis ©Louie Psihoyos/Science Faction
p.23 bottom; Getty Images/Andersen Ross **p.4**; Getty Images/Win
McNamee **p.5**; Getty Images/Time & Life Pictures **p.11**; Getty Images/
Time & Life Pictures **p.13**; Getty Images/Time & Life Pictures **p.14**;
Getty Images/Michal Czerwonka **p.17**; Getty Images/Ken Chernus
p.18; Getty Images/Adrian Weinbrecht **p.19**; Getty Images/Michael
Ochs Archives **p.21**; istockphoto ©John Clines **p.22**; Photolibrary/C Ray
Moore/Superstock **p.12**; The Granger Collection, New York **p.16**.

Cover photograph of Martin Luther King, Jr. addressing crowds during
the March On Washington at the Lincoln Memorial, Washington DC
reproduced with permission of Getty Images. Back cover photograph
reproduced with permission of Getty Images/Ken Chernus.

Every effort has been made to contact copyright holders of any material
reproduced in this book. Any omissions will be rectified in subsequent
printings if notice is given to the publisher.

Contents

What Is a Holiday?

A holiday is a special day.
People celebrate holidays.

Martin Luther King, Jr. Day is a holiday.
Martin Luther King, Jr. Day is in January.

Slavery and Segregation

Long ago, most black Americans were slaves. They had no rights.

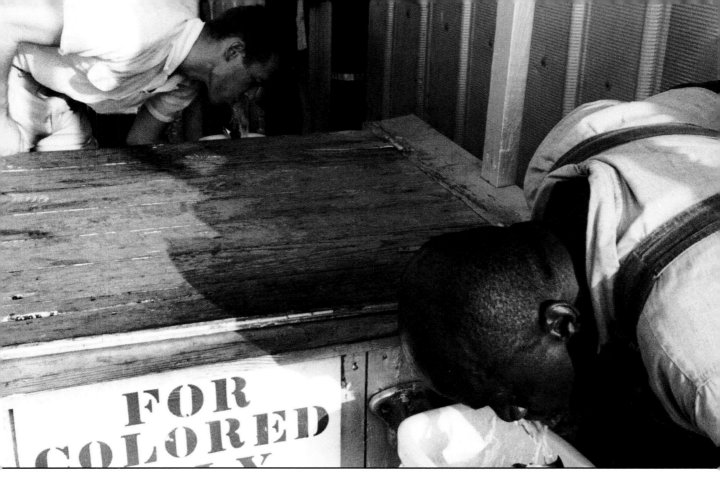

After slavery, black Americans were segregated. They were kept separate from other Americans.

Who Was Martin Luther King, Jr.?

Martin Luther King, Jr. lived in Atlanta, Georgia. Atlanta was segregated.

Black people in Atlanta could not go to the same places as white people.

Martin Luther King, Jr. did not think segregation was right.

He studied religion. He became
a minister.

He spoke out against segregation.
He became a leader.

He told black Americans to stand up for their rights.

He gave a speech about freedom for black people. He said he dreamed that all people could live together in peace.

In 1968, a man killed Martin Luther King, Jr. People all over America were sad.

Martin Luther King, Jr. had helped end segregation. Black Americans were able to vote for the first time.

Martin Luther King, Jr.'s dream was beginning to come true.

Celebrating Martin Luther King, Jr. Day

On Martin Luther King, Jr. Day people do service for each other.

People help their communities.
People help their neighbors.

Martin Luther King, Jr. Day Symbols

Martin Luther King, Jr. said, "I have a dream." He said he dreamed that all people had the same rights.

This speech is a symbol of Martin Luther King, Jr. Day. It reminds people of freedom for all Americans.

21

Calendar

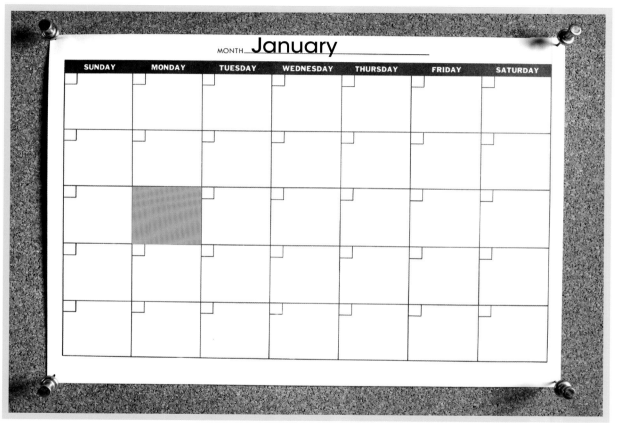

Martin Luther King, Jr. Day is the third Monday of January.

Picture Glossary

segregation when people are kept separate from others

slaves people who have no rights and work hard for others

Index

Note to Parents and Teachers

Before reading
Explain that every January, Americans recognize Martin Luther King, Jr. Day when we remember a brave leader in the fight for Civil Rights. Ask the children to share their thoughts on what it means to be treated fairly.

After reading
Share some of the lines from the "I Have a Dream" speech then ask the children to draw, write and share one of their dreams of how the world can be a more fair and just place.